The Lawyer Leader

Serve Authentically,
Find Peace, and Create Change

Ritu Goswamy, Esq.

ISBN 978-1-7375608-1-4 Digital Edition
ISBN 978-1-7375608-0-7 Paperback Edition

Cover Design: HR Hegnauer
Editing: Maggie McReynolds, Un-Settling Books
Author's photo courtesy of Maria Abelaye, HeartBox Photography

The Lawyer Leader

Advance Praise

In *The Lawyer Leader*, Ritu Goswamy shares invaluable advice I wish I had at the beginning of my legal career. Be yourself. Don't try to mimic other's behavior around you. I spent many years emulating lawyers around me. This inauthenticity led to untold stress and health issues. Learning to embrace my authenticity and listen to my inner voice led me to pursue a dual legal and business career. Ritu's advice and so much more in this book can help you have a genuine and authentic career experience and a healthier life.

—Sonya L. Sigler, Retired Lawyer, CEO PractiGal,
Author of *Welcome to the Next Level: 3 Secrets to Become Unstuck, Take Action, and Rise Higher in Your Career,*
and *What's Next for My Career?: Your Guide to Deciding to Leave Your Stable Job to Follow Your Passion*

Ritu's insights into relating to the law in a new way pave an easy path to becoming a lawyer leader via seven concise principles. Each one is very easy to contemplate and then act upon within the everyday challenges of lawyer life.

—Virginia Warren, Lawyer, Conflict Alchemist and
Author of *Let's Kiss All The Lawyers! ... Said No One Ever*

The Lawyer Leader is a great read! As attorneys it's easy to get caught up in the hustle and bustle and not take the time to do the things necessary to make us better practitioners. This book helped me refocus and recalibrate, and I can see myself reading it yearly as a means of re-energizing myself and my practice.

— Duane O. King, Esq., Author of *Stop Talking. Cut The Check.: Everything You Need to Know When You Get Injured in an Auto Accident*

Ritu's work is always well-researched and thoughtful. Building on their previous books, the author pulls together all the ingredients necessary for the road to becoming a complete lawyer. Not a lawyer that is based on the stereotypes and tropes that we have grown accustomed to, but one that knows themself, their responsibility, and how to execute on it.

—John Khosravi, Esq., President, Immigration Lawyers Toolbox®

This book is more than just techniques for effectively leading others. Rather, it is a practical guide for how to lead your own life by lightening your load, slowing down, and re-prioritizing, so that you have enough clarity to share your purpose and truest, "best self" with others. The heart-centered message of leading others with compassion and authenticity rather than imposition resonated with me, and I look forward to applying these mindful principles in my life and my law office.

—Nadeen Aljijakli, Esq.

Powerful, sincere, peaceful, and succinct. Ritu has a way of simply explaining the truth. Rooted in wisdom, this book walks you through its lessons to understand that the power to lead is within. A must-read if you are on the path to improving yourself and the way you practice law.

—Vilerka Solange Bilbao, Entrepreneur and Attorney

I have learned so much from each one of Ritu Goswamy's books. But T*he Lawyer Leader* spoke directly to me about my vocation, my calling, and my service to others as a lawyer. As a former bar leader and former career public servant, my compass has always pointed in the direction of service to others. *The Lawyer Leader* has sharpened my focus, reignited my passion for the practice of law as a means to engage in change, and given me a guidebook on how to return to and stay on the path. As I mentor less experienced lawyers, this book will be one that I give to each. It is a most refreshing, authentic "travel guide" for the lifetime journey of professionalism. I recommend every attorney read it each year as they prepare to review their past year and make plans for the next ... whenever and wherever that contemplation, inventory, and action planning takes place.

—Janine L. Rice, Esq.

This book on leadership shows attorney leaders how to analyze current steps, practices, and skills to then create new effective leadership skills of authentic service. Ritu Goswamy challenges attorneys to grow in self-awareness and to take inner work seriously because authentic growth starts from inside. This is a book for people who want to grow, and who desire to have a healthy, positive influence on others. Ritu provides seven principles of authenticity, creativity, centering, vulnerability, communication, self-integration, and presence to push lawyers towards mindfulness. The Lawyer Leader presents powerful tools for self-growth and for developing the skills of effective mindful leadership.

—Leslie Turnage, Esq.

Ritu's book is on point. The author highlights the need to develop a "better way of lawyering" and leading, which is precisely what the legal field needs. As the author points out, the traditional method of lawyering is outdated and needs a structural adjustment to the present times, especially in the way we lead as lawyers. This book elaborates on seven principles that will guide you in the process of reaching the highest levels of leadership and becoming a modern-day lawyer leader. *The Lawyer Leader* is not just a great book, but it is also a necessary read for today's lawyers.

—Brian Haderspock, LL.B

Table of Contents

For all the leaders past and present
who have shaped my life

and

In memory of Retired Judge David B. Moon Jr.,
who motivated me to keep writing

Foreword

Whether lawyers choose to be or want to be, lawyers are leaders! As leaders, we have to accept this truth by virtue of our education, training, and positions of responsibility we hold in our communities. But does having a legal education prepare lawyers to become effective leaders?

For almost thirty years, I have taught, trained, and mentored hundreds of law students. I have designed, directed, and consulted with academic support programs at several ABA law schools. I also train students and lawyers, informally and formally, to accept the responsibility of leadership. The State Bar of California created an Access & Fairness Leadership Academy (AFLA) to provide annual leadership training to a dozen attorneys from diverse backgrounds who wanted to serve underserved communities. I developed the lessons and taught most of the sessions along with established leaders in the legal profession.

Ritu Goswamy was a Leadership Scholar in AFLA for the 2006–07 year. After Ritu completed the program, we have remained connected and I continue to celebrate their accomplishments. Ritu is consistently authentic in their service to others, using both lived and professional experience and training to share their gift of leadership with lawyers in innovative ways. Ritu has already authored two successful books, *The New Billable Hour* and *The Holistic Lawyer*. This third book, *The Lawyer Leader*, builds on that success.

I have read many books on leadership. This book stands out. While most leadership development books direct you to conform to a specific leadership model promoted by the author, this book instead encourages you to create your own unique leadership style that reflects who you really are. It guides you to find and create a leadership style that fits your values and reflects your life experiences. By being yourself, your audience will feel more comfortable with you and confident in your path. In turn, you will feel more authentic and true to yourself. And, most importantly, you will be able to accomplish the goals that you set out for yourself. This book is all about being you!

Ritu encourages and empowers you to go deeper to invent a leadership model that fits your authentic self. Every chapter ends with insightful questions to help you discover yourself. Lawyers at every stage need support in order to take that next leadership step. This book is that support. Well-written, concise, evocative, and heartening, this book will help any lawyer (and law student) connect to the lawyer leader within.

– Rodney O. Fong, Legal Educator

Introduction: Why Leadership?

A genuine leader is not a searcher for consensus,

but a molder of consensus.

– Martin Luther King, Jr.

As a lawyer, you are already in a role of tremendous power and influence. You worked hard to get here without (completely) losing your mind. Despite the inevitable day-to-day overwhelm of practicing law, you enjoy the challenge of solving problems. Now is your time to lead other lawyers, and the society at large, to a better, more sustainable future.

This is a journey few travel. Becoming a lawyer takes courage, ambition, patience, determination, confidence, and drive. Being a lawyer requires consistent strength and tenacity. Whether you're in the courtroom or in the conference room, you give it your all to fight for justice. You had to be a leader just to get here.

You have learned how to perform your role as lawyer from those who have come before you. This role is most basically played out in how you relate to your clients. Traditionally, the lawyer takes an authoritative stance. The lawyer wants the client to look up to them, to see them in a superior role. In this capacity, the lawyer is expected to know more than the client, even about things the client has yet to discover.

The authoritative lawyer role can unfortunately draw out controlling behavior: the lawyer controls where the relationship goes, and the clients acquiesce. This type of relationship makes the client dependent on the lawyer for major decisions in their life. The lawyer overextends, takes on the burdens of their client, and ends up resenting the relationship.

Underneath, the lawyer feels incompetent to take on the responsibility of having to know everything for the client. The lawyer and the client may engage in a dysfunctional relationship because the lawyer is rescuing or pleasing the client instead of empowering and leading them.

If you, the lawyer, do not feel comfortable meeting the client on an authentic level, you cannot lead them. You will constantly engage in a power struggle with your clients. Clients will try to overpower you, and you them. Yes, clients have the ultimate power over their cases, but they shouldn't be given the power to undermine your self-confidence or ability to lead.

This is why traditional legal practice does not allow for evolved leadership, and why traditional lawyers can't effectively lead us to the future of law. The future of law is to be present and engaged on a deeper level, even as you fight for what is right.

In order to fight, you must also have peace. When you're not grounded, it's difficult to find the clarity you need. Without clarity, you exhaust yourself trying to find the truth. Your judgment is clouded, and leadership requires the clarity of mind that comes from stability or peace. By serving authentically, you will find the peace needed to expand your leadership skills. The seemingly conflicting ideals of fighting for justice and striving for peace can and do coexist.

As a lawyer leader, you generate change in yourself that ripples out to the profession. You break old paradigms and create new ways of serving. By cultivating the courage to rock the boat, your efforts will not only make your own life more satisfying but will also help others. I'm talking about the sentiment in the oft-quoted line attributed to Indian lawyer, politician, social activist, and writer Mahatma Gandhi: "Be the change you wish to see in the world."

You are always leading. How you choose to live affects those around you. You must use your education, training, and experience as a lawyer to lead others to find a better and more effective way to practice law. Evolving your understanding of leadership will give you more inner peace and a greater ability to create sustaining change in the legal profession and in the world.

Chapter 1

Slowly Changing Historical Precedent

Struggle is a never-ending process.
Freedom is never really won,
you earn it and win it in every generation.

– Coretta Scott King

The legal system has a history we call precedent. As we make sense out of the laws – rules based on culture and custom at the time they are made – we bring our own contemporary perspective to how to interpret the past.

Historically, when conflicts arose, the lawyers of the time created rules of law for a problem-solving structure. This structure gradually became the foundation for our legal system, which continues to be interpreted by lawyers. Each generation of lawyers struggles to set the direction of laws to ensure equity and fairness for all.

We, as lawyers, have the power to change the direction of the future of the profession, regardless of the history and precedent. However, we should look to the past in order to shape the future. By standing in the tension between respecting the past and confronting the present, lawyers become modern-day warriors in the cause of truth and justice.

The opportunity to both protect and change the system is probably why you became a lawyer. Maybe you thought you would fight for social justice and assure fairness for your clients. Maybe you wanted to preserve tradition and protect history. Either way, guarding or expanding what came before requires that you respect the past.

The legal system is slow to change, and your role as lawyer can feel severely limited. You want to promise the world to your clients, but you have to work within the confines of the law. You have to rely on the framework laid before you. A precedent is something that precedes, or comes before, and your work as a lawyer is dictated by it.

This precedent, for the most part, determines whether you win or lose. Yes, you can meticulously research and put together a magnificent argument for precedent in your favor. You will likely win.

However, precedent is also the reason you will lose. Your particular case, no matter how sympathetic your facts, is beholden to the past. Your unique case must be compared to similar cases that came before. Then you get to play the game of distinguishing your arguments from bad precedent or showing likeness to good precedent.

This is the life of the lawyer. There is not much glamour or fame. It's just you and your precedent, struggling at times to make a difference. It can be frustrating to have to argue about small points of law that may have originated a couple hundred years ago. Instead of sweeping social reform and justice, our day-to-day world is, in fact, in the weeds of words.

The law is like a historical house we still live in. Let me give you an example from my life. As I write this chapter, we're experiencing a planned power outage. I've seen plenty of power outages before, and they usually come with their share of drama. Living in the mountains often means inclement weather, impassable roads, and lots of confusion. This morning, when I woke up, I knew the power would be out. I took my time with my morning routine.

I fished out my tiny camping stove, boiled myself some water, and added lemon. Then I built a fire in the wood-burning stove before I headed to my meditation cushion. After meditation, I did some writing, cooked some oats, and heated water for tea on the wood-burning stove.

Around midday, I added gasoline to my generator, got it going, and went through the steps to have it run the essential parts of my house – namely the refrigerator, septic pump, and internet. As I climbed down under my house built on stilts to exchange one of the plugs, I had a deep realization that every single part of my house, and of my life, had a history.

The house was built a certain way. Over the years, additional amenities were added to make it work better. Some parts are state-of-the-art technology – and others are so basic it's mystifying that these tools and systems still work.

I reveled at how the world operates – what we use for fuel, how we create electricity, how we handle waste and preserve our food. I pondered how I could not work on (or in) my business without the internet. It was fascinating.

The practice of law is just this! The laws and structures of our society were formed at a previous time in history, based on what was then needed. Most have sustained the test of time, but many have crumbled due to their obsolete and often discriminatory nature. Some laws had flexibility built in. The US Constitution was meant to be a living document and continuously open to improvement.

Lawyers are constantly testing the laws to see if they are still viable and just. We strive to assure that our clients are treated fairly. If the law is not fair to our client, we challenge it. It is what we do.

Over time, we have used history and precedent as a basis to create the legal system. Much like I worked with my editor to shape this book, lawyers shape the law with each new case. How glorious and delightful to have a profession (and calling) that not only helps solve your client's problem but also affects those who will have the same problem in the future.

While challenging a dysfunctional system requires a fight, the imperfect structures do provide us with a foundation. From there, we can imagine improvements. The legal system assures that we progress as a society based on undeniable truths and values. These values can be misinterpreted, but the spirit lives on.

The spirit of precedent is that we cannot move forward without affirming the past. But sometimes we hold onto the past a little too tightly and become afraid of change. We want to evolve, and yet the unknown is frightening.

What if, in our quest for progress, we lose? Oh, I am putting into words our biggest fear! What if we make things worse in the attempt to make it better? Then not only is our client affected but also, perhaps, future clients. This is not a good situation. We don't want to even consider harming anyone, much less do it on purpose.

At this point you may be spinning with the terror of malpractice and ethics violations. Take a deep breath, settle down, and read on.

Let's step back and consider the weight we lawyers carry when we challenge precedent. It is truly a burden. Of course, we would tell others (on some days) that we welcome that burden as a badge of honor. The opportunity to fight is why we are here, isn't it? When stakes are high, we are motivated to do our best.

But what about when we win? Winning a difficult case is the biggest satisfaction a lawyer could feel. When we win in a way that helps our client and makes good law for those after us – we have arrived. All of the angst and near-burnout was worth it. We earned our privilege to be a lawyer. We feel powerful and smart and capable. We are ready for the next challenge and opportunity to change the law. After we recover, of course.

All this emotional upheaval and mental exhaustion definitely takes its toll. Our physical and mental health are literally attacked by work. We sacrifice taking care of our bodies and minds to serve our clients. Going into overdrive destroys our nervous system, and our mental health becomes unstable.

We cope with our unhealthy bodies and minds with self-destructive behaviors such as substance abuse, overworking, and neglecting relationships or isolating. These coping mechanisms lead to more damage and usually result in the anxiety and depression that most of us assume is unavoidable.

The real tragedy is that, in the downward spiral, we lose connection to ourselves. This is a deeper cost of being a lawyer. We are no longer in alignment with our purpose. All human beings need a purpose, a reason to get up in the morning. For some it is the relationships in our lives, for others it is the self-expression we share with the world.

For lawyers, it is our ability to facilitate future change while honoring the past. Our purpose is to help the legal system move forward. Even though the system was not built by us, or by people like us, it's our turn to shape it for the future.

How do we take on this challenge? There is a different way to be a lawyer that is more creative and visionary and does not end up in burnout. Instead of fighting exhaustively, how about changing the underlying paradigm? That change may seem impossible, but the system we now have is broken. Lawyers themselves are breaking down.

You can change the legal system by relating to it in a new way. And you know what happens when you relate to something in a new way? It starts to shift for the better. This is how you will change the legal system as a lawyer leader. Keep reading, and I'll show you how.

Chapter 2

Challenging the Status Quo: My Lawyer Leader Journey

If they don't give you

a seat at the table,

bring a folding chair.

– Shirley Chisholm

Growing up, I was taught to do what I was told. Success meant upholding the status quo and conforming to the expectations of others. I am a child of immigrants, and striving for achievement was valued and respected by my family's culture. I learned that following the rules got me external validation and praise, and I got really good at it.

But following external rules did not align with what I wanted inside. I secretly wanted to break the rules. I wanted to challenge the status quo to improve my life and help others.

To manage the tension between honoring my family and meeting my own needs, I chose to become a lawyer. The career path in law meant I could both appease my parents' idea of success and learn about how to change the system from the inside.

I knew that the rules I meticulously followed were based on a paradigm that was antiquated and built to elevate only certain groups of people. But I also knew that in order to change that paradigm, I needed to learn how it functioned. For me, becoming a lawyer meant earning a position of leadership from which I could create change.

My first lawyer job, twenty years ago, was my dream job at the time. I was doing influential work with esteemed colleagues under the direction of a respected supervisor. Despite my lack of experience as a lawyer, I was put in a major leadership role immediately. I was trusted with important duties for the firm. I felt valued for my passion, ambition, and skills.

I welcomed the responsibility of creating change, but I was entering a traditional profession built by people who did not necessarily want it to change quickly. I had to quickly learn the law that I was charged with changing. I was expected to have a handle on the body of law and precedent, and also be ready with multi-faceted strategies to improve it. Looking back, that sounds exciting. While it was happening, however, it was terrifying.

Plenty of work needed to be done, and I felt unable to keep up. Unfortunately, I already didn't fit into the expected model of a lawyer. Instead of sucking it up, I pushed back when the demands were not reasonable. I spoke up when I was struggling.

My struggle at work resulted in serious talks with my supervisor, who ultimately gave me a warning and suggested that maybe practicing law was not for me. They explained that there were many other things I could do with my law degree. I don't think they meant their comments to be harmful. They were likely trying to help me. They were showing me the way they'd succeeded in their own career.

But their way was not for me. I resigned from that job and continued to forge my path in law differently. Instead of giving up, I stood up for myself and my future in the profession. My determination to do law my way was an early example of my being a lawyer leader.

In my next job, I created a lifestyle that suited me while still complying with my professional requirements. I was in a wonderful work environment, and my colleagues were smart and motivated. I was able to have a voice and take on leadership roles.

I had a work-life balance that included self-care. My work was fulfilling and meaningful. I was respected and valued for what I had to offer. I spoke up, and constantly made changes in the way I practice law. I led initiatives for change in the workplace.

When I mastered that work environment, I sought out new challenges for leadership.

My legal career includes creating a legal services program for former gang members and at-risk youth; establishing and growing my own immigration law firm; developing a parallel health and wellness career; becoming a published author (twice), and founding my current consulting business where I am a Lawyer Leadership Coach and DEI (Diversity, Equity, and Inclusion) Strategist.

I present this list of accomplishments to demonstrate that lawyer leadership is a personal journey. Think about your own journey to see how you got to this place in your career.

I have had external guides in the form of mentors, books, teachers, and coaches. But my main guide has been my own internal voice. I have learned that leadership isn't just about following the rules. Leadership is about learning which rules to break or change by listening to that inner voice.

By allowing my inner guide to lead me, I create positive change. Thus, my lawyer leadership journey has become intertwined with my personal growth. When I get stuck, I challenge myself to work through it. Each breakthrough elevates my level of leadership.

Reader, I wrote this book to facilitate *your* next breakthrough in lawyer leadership.

Chapter 3

Levels of Lawyer Leadership

Do the best you can

until you know better.

Then when you know better,

do better.

– Maya Angelou

I had always wanted to learn a martial art and chose aikido for its beauty and spiritual aspects. I liked that participants were not opponents but partners in this art of peace.

I wasn't interested in eventually earning a belt. I practiced aikido so I could learn to better get along with others. When it came time to sign up for my exam, I wasn't enthusiastic. I didn't want to trivialize the spirit I brought to my practice. I had managed thus far to hold my practice lightly, which for a lawyer and ambitious person like me was challenging. I just wanted to practice and train and learn at my own pace. I didn't want to take an exam, be tested, show off, or rely on external validation.

When I told a few fellow aikido practitioners I trusted that I didn't want to take the exam, they explained that if I had been asked, I had already passed. They shared that they were nervous about their exams, too, and didn't like taking it publicly. But that part didn't bother me. I was happy to perform and show others what I had learned. I was thrilled that we primarily learn by watching others. Then what was my problem? I took some time to get quiet and listen to why I was getting in my own way. Why was I making such a big deal about this – at least in my head?

After some thought, I realized that the martial arts exams were not exams at all – not the way lawyers have experienced exams. The belt "exam" is a ceremony, a rite of passage, an opportunity to show everyone (and yourself) that you are ready to move on to the next level of training. In watching other people's exams, I was heartened to see that their preparation for the exam was the most crucial part.

For preparation, the community comes together and offers help. We deepen existing relationships, and new ones surface. When I made the choice to wholeheartedly prepare for my first exam, everything changed for the better. My practice got even lighter. With the help of my aikido friends, I took risks. I cleaned up edges. I became more graceful and open-hearted. I got curious about what I knew and didn't know. I became more confident and grateful. Most of all, I embraced my role of moving up, or getting promoted, in my practice as an example to other beginning students. Training for a test meant I was committed to growth and continued learning. It meant that I was willing to put myself out there and also celebrate the effort I'd been putting in.

The levels in martial arts symbolize the levels of life. You may have learned about the stages of human development in school. Even if you didn't, you know that from birth, through childhood, and into adolescence, there were significant milestones in your life. I bet some surely felt like exams. Some were definitely public. Most of them required that you reach out for help from those who had gone before you. Then you became an adult when the actual examinations did begin. I don't want to drag you back to the SAT, college, the LSAT, law school, the bar exam – wait, sorry, I just did.

My point is that those exams or milestones were important for both you and me to get here to this point in time. Once we became lawyers, the ceremony of the exams or milestones mostly slipped away. We were thrown into a profession where community and celebration are not valued. We have been spending our days (and nights) in an adversarial world where we are constantly criticizing (and being criticized by) other people. We are striving and ambitious, and trying to excel for our clients, bosses, and judges. So when milestones come, we may not even notice them. That means we may not even know that we are at a higher level or stage. We keep old habits and continue to slog through. We don't even take a moment to notice, celebrate, and enjoy our personal and professional development.

In my research for this book, I had the opportunity to interview many lawyers of different ages, legal experience, and areas of law practice. I simply put out there that I wanted to interview lawyers about leadership for a book I was writing. Many lawyers stepped up to help. I was amazed at the breadth and depth of knowledge and insight these lawyers had about what it means to be a leader, especially for a lawyer. I was impressed and moved by how these lawyers were committed to leave a legacy of improving the lives of others. You'll see quotes from those lawyer leader interviews throughout this book.

However, the lawyers I interviewed didn't know about the research on levels of leadership. The lawyers were very clear about where they were currently in their leadership skills and how far they had come. They also acknowledged that there was work they needed to do on their leadership skills and were seeking out help via books and coaches. But they didn't see the link between their own stages of personal development and their level of leadership.

In personal or human development, we move through adulthood in stages. The adult stages of development are the crux of leading others. The following leadership framework is the basis of the research by Bill Joiner and Stephen Josephs in their book *Leadership Agility: Five Levels of Mastery for Anticipating and Initiating Change*. I have adapted the descriptions of the levels to apply to lawyer leaders.

The Conformer

The first adult stage is the Conformer stage, which likely begins in middle school. Preadolescents have a basic ability for abstract thought and to imagine how they are seen by others. This is when we learn how to conform to society's conventions of what we are supposed to be. Some people remain in this stage for their entire lives.

The Expert

In the Expert level, leaders are motivated by developing subject-matter expertise. They assume that a leader's legitimate power comes from expertise and positional authority. This level was established in law school, and how you may have approached being a baby lawyer. Expert level lawyer leaders are prepared. They look for authority outside themselves before they can commit to having authority themselves.

They lead by telling others what to do based on what they already know. They value themselves in a support role for other lawyers. Expert level lawyers have a strong problem-solving orientation and the ability to think independently and analytically.

In order to move beyond the Expert level of leadership, the lawyer needs to step back from narrow problem-solving to develop their own system of values and beliefs.

The Achiever

The next stage is the Achiever stage, marked by development of a strong identity and a system of values, beliefs, and goals to live by. This is where we find highly successful professionals, including lawyers, who have a strong sense of their role in the world. It's definitely a platform from which to lead others and make a difference in the world.

The Achiever level leaders have deepened their capacity for self-reflection. The Achiever lawyer leader learns from their past experiences. They realize that a leader's power comes from motivating others. Achievers have a stronger capacity for strategic thinking. At this level, lawyers start their own firms, and also take on leadership positions in organizations in the legal profession and the community.

Achievers likely have causes they support and values they stand by. They want to teach and lead others from a deeper place of knowledge. They genuinely want to help their staff and clients to succeed. They are motivated by motivating others. Achiever level lawyers are also interested in practicing law with integrity. They want to hold themselves out as a lawyer that clients can trust. They care about their reputations. They want to do a good job and help others in the process.

For managers of corporations, the research by Joiner and Josephs finds that 10 percent are at the Conformer level, 45 percent at the Expert level, and 35 percent at the Achiever level. There is a similar pattern among lawyers. Lawyers are likely to toggle between the Expert and Achiever levels of leadership.

Expert level lawyers are problem-solvers and use their expertise and authority (which they build with time). They are the supervisors, and they lead teams based on what they know. Achiever level lawyers, however, are interested in what others have to say and teach. They will accept feedback and even initiate it if it will help their outcomes. These lawyer leaders can adapt to different environments in order to achieve an outcome.

I am sure your lawyer brain is trying to make sense of this and dutifully deciding where you fit in. The thing is that even if you are an Achiever, you are bound to fall back on the previous levels. For example, as a baby we learned to walk and talk; we don't forget those levels of development as adults. Similarly, we had to learn in the Conformer stage how to conform with societal norms in order to become lawyers and understand the context within which we work and live. As Experts, we have to continually develop our expertise and authority as lawyers to hone our craft. From those foundations, we can consider how to motivate others for a desired outcome as Achievers.

Just as the levels that came before are always with us as we progress, the next level is always within our reach, if we pay attention and increase our awareness. When we can focus, we see that mastering each level and feeling that there must be more is an indicator that it is time to level up. In other words, when we reach success as we have defined it, there may be a feeling of emptiness toward what is next. That is the time to progress to the next level. Just like my preparation for my aikido exam began the day I walked into the dojo and signed up for classes, your journey into the highest levels of lawyer leadership began when you decided to go to law school.

Yes, I said the highest levels of lawyer leadership. In Joiner and Josephs' framework, there are three rare, high-level stages of leadership after the Achiever level. These levels are called the Catalyst, the Co-creator, and the Synergist.

The Catalyst

The Catalyst was only found in 5 percent of those leaders studied. They are visionary and believe that leaders articulate an innovative, inspiring vision and bring together the right people to transform the vision into reality. Catalyst lawyer leaders pay attention to current experience, reflect on it immediately, and adjust their response accordingly. This process requires awareness of their values and beliefs.

The Co-creator

The Co-creator accounted for 4 percent of the leaders. They are oriented toward shared purpose and collaboration. They believe that leadership is ultimately a service to others. Co-creator lawyer leaders know how to invoke a state of flow that comes from being in the present moment. They are able to intentionally enter into the flow state even while in mentally complex and emotionally charged situations.

The Synergist

The Synergist is quite rare – only 1 percent in those studied were at this level of leadership. They have a holistic orientation and experience leadership as their life purpose that benefits others while serving their own personal transformation. The Synergist lawyer leader is both alert and relaxed in present-centered awareness. Their present experience becomes so vibrant that wherever they happen to focus stands out sharply from its background. They just want to experience all of life at its fullest, while living in their purpose.

There are some extraordinary visionary leaders geared to collaboration and shared purpose. The highest-level leaders are aware that they must step down from wanting to be the authority and believe that leadership is a service to others. They are holistic in that they do not separate their work and personal life from their life purpose. They use their vocation as a vehicle for personal transformation and for the transformation of others.

These high-level ideas can be overwhelming and perhaps burdensome. For me, it brings an awareness of a huge responsibility that I have as a lawyer. As I explained, it does not matter where you are in your personal and professional journey. I wrote this book to help you understand and grow from wherever you are. As a lawyer leader, I provide you with a resource for when you are ready to level up. Since you are still reading, you are ready for more right now.

In this book I will lay out seven principles that I've created to give you the tools to stay on the path to the highest levels of lawyer leadership. As a lawyer, you have the foundation, expertise, authority, and ambition to be a high-level leader and to help heal this planet. I commend you for being open to how you can evolve your skills and move to *your* next level of lawyer leadership.

You may feel a tug back to your old habits and ways as you explore the concepts and principles I put forward. That's understandable. I am going to make arguments that will be new and foreign to the way you may have been taught to lead. The principles may seem irrelevant to what you think leadership and success means. You may be focused on building and scaling your law firm and measuring success by the bottom line of income earned and clients served. You may have your plate full by taking on leadership positions in your bar associations, chamber of commerce, and your children's schools. You may be supervising and mentoring younger lawyers and teaching them in the way you wish you were taught. I know that you are doing all these things, and I don't want you to stop.

I just ask that you open up a pathway to consider that there is another piece to lawyer leadership, success, and professional contentment. I propose that the nagging feeling you have underneath it all is a calling to learn more. You can grow yourself to the next level of leadership, and the world needs you to do so.

I hope to strike a chord with you to enhance the leadership skills you already have. It is time to level up not only your own career and life but also the practice of law. Our profession hangs at a precipice. Are we going to let it self-destruct, or do we step in with a new vision for client service, professional expertise, and conflict resolution?

I know that you are already quietly wondering how you can do things better. You also may be afraid of how you will come across to other lawyers, judges, and clients. We must respect and preserve tradition. We will simply adjust who we are as lawyers and people. Let's truly make the difference in the world, a difference we were meant to make as lawyers.

I truly believe that, as lawyers, we can change the world for the better. Lawyers are at the forefront of conflict, and well-positioned to heal and transform it. I envision a world where lawyers are confident, empowered, generous, collaborative leaders for our clients and society at large. I cannot carry out this vision without you. Please consider this book as an invitation to change the paradigm of practicing law into one that is sustainable, healing, and satisfying. If you want to love your job and use it as a way to make the world a better place while making a good living and remaining in integrity with your values and beliefs, join me.

Chapter 4

Principle One: Authenticity

Defining myself,

as opposed to being defined by others,

is one of the most difficult challenges I face.

– Carol Moseley-Braun

Discovering your authentic self is a challenging endeavor. In your life, you may have inadvertently relied on others to define who you should be. This can lead to pretending to be someone that others expect. The performance can work for a while – until you start feeling like an imposter.

The legal profession is marred with a phenomenon called imposter syndrome. Imposter syndrome occurs when someone doubts their accomplishments and lives in fear of being exposed as a fraud. People who suffer from this thought pattern feel their successes are unearned and attribute them to luck. This syndrome can manifest with constant feelings of anxiety, stress, and depression.

Imposter syndrome is a result of being conditioned to perform, rather than embody, a role. In the practice of law, using a performative lawyer mask is common. And behind that dramatic lawyer mask can lurk the mental health and substance abuse problems in the profession that are now coming to light.

If you're suffering quietly (even occasionally) from feelings of self-doubt and diminished self-confidence, you're not alone. The feeling that others must know more than you has sadly become part of being a lawyer regardless of individual background, and does not disappear over time.

One of my coaching clients is a successful attorney of

over twenty years. Even though most of the time they are self-confident, they still sometimes feel like they are not a good lawyer. When their clients' insecurities cause mistrust and aggressive communication, this lawyer's self-doubt comes up.

Feelings of self-doubt can also be rooted not in fear of failure, but in fear of success. Yes, you read that right. Imposters feel guilt for having opportunities, education, and accomplishments others do not. Lawyers can feel especially guilty about their position relative to others.

Those feelings of guilt reinforce imposter syndrome. Instead of taking off the lawyer mask, we continue to hide behind it, often because we don't feel like we deserve success. Lawyers may pretend to be omniscient because we think clients expect this of us. But even when clients give up their power to authority figures, is that what they really want?

You put on the lawyer mask to serve your clients, perhaps because you believe you're meeting their expectations by doing so, or because you perceive they want separation from you. Worse, creating separation can trigger your imposter syndrome. I offer another perspective. The client actually wants authenticity.

Are you getting my drift, here? Let's change direction from imposter to authentic service. This shift will launch you into the higher levels of leadership I presented earlier. In this book, I offer you seven lawyer leader principles that will help you find peace in yourself and create change around you. The principles that follow are anchored in the concept of authenticity.

Being authentic is easier said than done. That's why I am here with you to guide you, step by step, through your personal and professional development. You are destined to become a lawyer leader and make your impact. It all starts with serving authentically. When you are authentic, it is not possible to be an imposter. Authenticity remedies your imposter syndrome.

Clients (and everyone else in your life) want you to be authentic. Even if they don't fully recognize it, people want a lawyer who is real and not hiding behind a lawyer mask. Clients hire lawyers to get through challenging times in their lives. They are often emotional and mistrustful, and they want a lawyer who will tell them the truth. Remember those times when your clients were grateful for your honesty?

> "One the biggest mistakes young lawyers make is trying to put on a [lawyer] mask and be somebody else, to do a trial like they've seen on TV or seen someone else do, instead of just being really your

own self. It's okay to make mistakes; in fact, a lot of times it's more endearing to a jury if you do make a mistake in front of them. You don't have to be over the top apologetic, but you can say, 'I screwed up; I am human.' And they like that because they are too."

– Lawyer Leader Interview

Honesty is authentic. Just like you authenticate an official document to prove it's not falsified, you are in the process of authenticating *yourself*. Authenticity is the degree to which your actions are congruent with your beliefs and desires, despite external pressures. Be genuine. Be real. There is no fraud in being real. Authenticity unmasks the imposter. Imposter syndrome simply cannot exist if you are being yourself.

Since imposter syndrome is based on guilt, insecurities, and lies, being true to yourself is the cure. Authenticity is the beginning of an even deeper, more fulfilling life and career.

Instead of imitating what others have done, you forge your own path. Many lawyers I have spoken with are eager to learn how someone else succeeded so they can replicate that success. There are many leadership and business books telling the stories of leaders and how they have done it. This information is useful, of course. But how can you really be authentic if you're chasing after someone else's dream?

In my direct work with my coaching clients, I understand the atrophy of the muscle to envision what they truly want. They, and you, have the natural capability to dream. The dreamer in you has been hindered by your lawyer mask.

The lawyer mask creates separation from others and from yourself. As baby lawyers, you may have started out playing the role of the aggressive and intimidating lawyer. Over time, this lawyer mode has led to burnout, health problems, and deep dissatisfaction with your career. Being a lawyer became less meaningful and you may have forgotten why you did all this. The good news is that you are here now, and it is time to take your next step.

What's next for you? How about taking off the mask? How about being courageous enough to put your true self out there? Here's the thing you might not already know. Putting your authentic genuine self out there is the true path to leadership. It's one thing to be an expert or a high-achieving professional. It's another thing to rock the boat, talk about your work in a revolutionary way, and create pathways to success that didn't exist before. This is the way you will step into the role of a lawyer leader and make your legacy.

You are probably at the edge of your seat wondering, "How do I be authentic?!" Good question. You're in good hands because I have some guidance for you. The most difficult part of being authentic is avoiding the distraction of what others are doing. While it may be useful to know how others express themselves and their missions, be careful not to compare or get discouraged.

Avoiding comparison is something I work on all the time. For you, it's not about putting in more effort, but about being you. Remember that you have something unique to offer. Even if you are feeling shaky and confused, take a step forward. Then take another. Just like learning to walk, learning to authentically lead is a process.

You will fall down; you will meet resistance. Your job is to gently bring yourself back. Keep your foundation strong by establishing daily lifestyle routines to keep yourself focused and less distracted. In order to focus, you must be self-aware, or mindful. Mindfulness is a requirement for anyone who wants to lead and stay focused on their goals. I personally get distracted easily and don't know what I would do without my mindfulness and meditation practices to keep a baseline of stability in my life.

Telling you how to establish your own mindfulness practices would take an entire book. In fact, it took two, which is why I already wrote them. *The New Billable Hour* and *The Holistic Lawyer* contain systems and processes for how to deepen mindfulness practices for you and your law firm. Rather than repeat all that information here, you can find more information at www.ritugoswamy.com.

> "As a law firm owner, I had absolutely been killing myself to do certain things and to accomplish certain goals. I watched my health decline, and am still dealing with the ramifications. I have had to make time to take regular walks every day even though I think I should be billing for an hour, not walking. I have had to get my head in a better place. I have been doing guided meditations. I have been trying to be more intentional and seeing how to make our firm such that we are bringing our best selves into our work, and leaving enough of our best selves for our family."
>
> – Lawyer Leader Interview

While it's important to have role models and mentors, we should remember that each of us is a unique person. Replicating other people's successes could work for a while. But when you try to mimic what worked for someone else, you may only get short-term results. Ultimately, you will be propelled back to your same habits and challenges. Just because someone else's journey led them to learn shortcuts and methods to their dreams doesn't mean you get to skip your own journey. This journey of being authentic is a long, twisty, arduous one. I am not going to lie. (Lying would be inauthentic, anyway.)

Notice I wrote journey *of* being authentic, not journey *to*. As you have likely heard many times before, it's not about the destination. You are on a journey called life. You are literally moving from one thing to the next for your entire existence.

Even in your last breaths, you are still on the journey of being authentic. This may be disturbing news, that being authentic is a life-long exercise and effort. Or maybe you feel some relief that you have plenty of time? Either way, with each breath, each step, each decision, each mistake, and each success, you are moving along your own unique path.

Some parts of the journey are fantastically amazing. You have already experienced so much success and happiness, I am sure. Some parts will actually be quite mundane. Then there the parts that some would argue are the most important – the really challenging ones that just tear your heart open. Don't pretend you don't know what I'm talking about. Seriously, there are times you just can't understand why you're even doing this. What is the point? Why you?

If you can connect your head, heart, and gut, you will be better able to ride out those times. If you choose to separate yourself by distractions or denial, it will be a harder trip. Either way, you will get to the other side, I promise. I am sure of it because you have done it many times before. The evidence of your evolution is your readiness to read this book.

Feeling blessed with too much opportunity for growth in your journey of being authentic? Rest assured that if you cultivate awareness around those rough patches, you will be able to evolve very quickly into higher levels of personal, professional, and leadership growth.

You are living in a time where it is less shameful to heal your past. You may have participated in psychotherapy. You may have read self-help books, taken courses, attended events, or worked with a coach or consultant. If you are lucky, you've used difficult times in your life to help others.

As I write to the lawyer leaders out there, I know that I must stay on my own path. I must continue to forge forward and learn who I am now and who I want to be. I, dear reader, am directly on my own journey of being authentic.

Just because people tell me that I'm already authentic doesn't mean my work is done. It just means that I'm on the right track. You will see this too. When you lift off your lawyer mask, even slowly, others will get glimpses of you.

They will be drawn to you. Opportunities will come to you. Distractions will fall away.

It seems too good to be true, doesn't it? The more you invest in turning inward, in getting to know yourself, the more the outside world will fall into place. It is not an easy switch. It is far from it. You will forget more often than you would like. You will have to remember again and again to take off the mask after you put it back on. Believe me, I know.

Authenticity not only remedies imposter syndrome, but it puts you on a journey to find your way. Instead of replicating, you will create. You will lead from a place of authentic service, and impact others in a way you didn't even know was possible.

By choosing, over and over again, to be your imperfect perfect self, you are choosing to be a lawyer leader. You are choosing to step into the most satisfying and challenging role of your life. I suspect you wouldn't have it any other way. I know I wouldn't.

> "Leadership is being the authentic person, dropping that façade, dropping the belief that we have to have that front on all the time, no matter where we are – because we don't have to. There is this stigma against that in the legal field of showing any emotion or

> showing compassion. But when you come down to it, that's what clients want, it's what your staff wants. That's what anyone coming to you for advice wants. They don't want you to be like, 'Just suck it up and deal with it.' They want you to have compassion; they want to know you understand and hear them. Even if I am giving them advice that they don't like, I am doing it compassionately and listening to them. I hear them."
>
> – Lawyer Leader Interview

Your turn! At the end of each chapter, you will be guided to do an internal contemplation and an external action, so you can have a taste of what my clients do in my coaching programs. Some of my clients like to write this all out, but it's fine to just hold these questions in your head and notice what arises.

Internal Contemplation

Journal or contemplate the following questions:

1. What choices have you made because you thought you should?

2. Who are you without a lawyer mask on?

3. How can you be more authentic in your daily life?

External Action

Create (or revise) your law firm's Mission Statement to be more authentic.

Chapter 5

Principle Two: Creativity

Not everything that is faced can be changed,

but nothing can be changed until it is faced.

–James Baldwin

With everything moving so fast, how can you keep up? Modern culture rewards speed. Moreover, people give irrational respect to those who move quickly and appear to be busy. As a lawyer, you may feel like you are always chasing your mountain of paperwork, calls and emails to respond to, legal updates to read, and cases to review. But there just isn't enough time to catch any of it!

I recently made a vow to stop chasing or be chased. Of course, this promise is one I have to make repeatedly. It helps me bring awareness to how I approach my work. If I am lucky enough to notice that I'm trying to grab a client, project, or opportunity, I take a breath and slow that train (of thought) down.

You are ambitious and creative. As a lawyer, you're creating the law that is about to be. You are also creating your dreams. Once you achieve a goal, you want to go after the next one. This is an accepted and productive way to live. However, are you really living? Are you paying attention to the process?

The second lawyer leader principle is creativity. You will create change by moving slowly. This requires self-confidence. It requires acceptance of all the unfinished tasks in your life right now. Looking back, you know that some of those tasks will get done, and, frankly, most won't. In fact, the in-between stage of *thinking* you have to do them will distract you from the things you will do. You will achieve great success whether or not you catch up with your tasks.

My coaching client posted this on social media:

> "As a law student, I dreamt of becoming a lawyer one day so that I could represent folks that could use someone on their side. Before going to law school I did not know, or know of, a Latina lawyer. Much less one that had their own law practice. Now I am recognized as Solo Attorney of the Month by a magazine for my work providing access to immigration law with dignity. I want you to know, and share this – because 'if you can see it, you can be it.' It may be your dream to own your own business or something else. I want you to know that you reach your goals one step at a time, when no one is watching."

Pursue your dreams one step at a time. When you chase your thought train, knowing full well you cannot catch it, you can spin out of control. In your effort to control a situation, you lose that very control by running after it quickly. It feels like, if you move faster, talk faster, attempt to multitask, and learn shortcuts and hacks, then you can get somewhere faster.

In fact, lawyer culture reinforces the illusion that if you slow down, you may get behind. But you are already behind when you chase! Lawyers are even called ambulance chasers. What if, instead of chasing, you move to a slower roll and sidle up to what is most important to you? What if you gradually get closer instead of being behind the next shiny object, or file of documents?

> "Being a lawyer leader is stepping away and knowing when you can't do something, or when you shouldn't be doing something. A lawyer leader sets an example for other lawyers."
>
> – Lawyer Leader Interview

If you are feeling behind or lost or overwhelmed or stressed or inadequate or exhausted, this means it's time to slow down. Usually, when you feel overwhelmed, you don't want to get more behind. So you inefficiently try to go even faster through your tasks. This tactic ultimately doesn't work.

Unexpectedly, to get more done, you must slow down. Slowing down is the way you keep up. When you slow down, you can better handle your tasks and stay focused on your goals.

Instead of being oriented toward results, engage in the process. Do one thing at a time mindfully. Spend more quiet time with yourself to tap into your own intuitive ability. Avoid spending too much time with the task if it is not moving forward. Leave the task alone. While it can be helpful to understand what others are doing, avoid getting pulled in so much that you get distracted. Your inner voice has the answer you need to get unstuck, and it can get drowned out by the outside noise.

> "My biggest challenge is expectation of myself as well those around me. I like to pride myself on thinking that I don't ask for more than I would ask of myself. But I recognize that my bar is very high. I need to be mindful of that to avoid disappointing myself, and to inject some realism into my expectations."
>
> – Lawyer Leader Interview

I am telling you to slow down, lean in, feel the tension, and get next to it. Don't wait for everything outside of you to slow down.

As I write this chapter, I am in the middle of December, when my external world is spiraling fast to the end of the year. During this season, I hope for moments of calm as I end the year and start the next. I am always surprised that the year-end and year-beginning are literally consecutive! There is no gap on the calendar, no winding down before revving up. Here I am, writing this chapter and remembering that it is me who must wind down.

A client in my Lawyer Leader coaching program shared this on social media at year-end:

"Even though I'm really afraid of heights, I've always pushed my mind to the limit, forcing myself to climb higher. I've spent years fighting with my thoughts, competing with my mind and all the crazy ideas I have in there. But this year I decided to stop trying to control myself, others, and all things beyond my control.

"Every day I work on trying to accept things as they are and not struggle against them. I love the adrenaline, I love the high, and that attitude has totally defined my life up until this year. As this year comes to an end, I'm so grateful that I've learned to observe myself from a different angle. Instead of always chasing the rush, I'm at a place that allows me to feel more calmness, more contentment, and more confidence."

There will never be an experience outside of you that will help you stop chasing. You will always have the thought that you must visualize the next thing right now. You may be hearing marketing messages about how to reach your goals faster and get immediate results. The experts want to teach you about their shortfalls so you can skip them and get to the finish line faster. However, life is not a sprint, but a marathon.

Mentors can guide you to stay focused on your own long-term goals. While mentorship is crucial to know where you are going, you are still on your own journey.

As I cultivate my own creative abilities, I find pacing more of an issue. I produce content more often than ever, and I have to continually remind myself to slow down. This slowing down is crucial for my mission of helping you, dear lawyer, change the legal profession.

If you try to change things too fast, you'll crash in your attempts. But if you approach the endeavor with a slow grace, magic will happen. Slowing down for lasting change has been modeled by some great teachers and leaders.

> "Part of being a leader is knowing what you can and can't handle, or what you are not willing to sacrifice. My family and my mental health are key."
>
> – Lawyer Leader Interview

As you stay in the legal profession, you must have activities in your life that remind you that slowing down leads to more successful change. My journey with slow movement has included yoga, qigong, and aikido, to challenge me to slow down. When I relax, I can access more of myself. I don't feel like I am chasing. I feel like I have already arrived.

Wouldn't you like to feel you're there already? That place where you can lead and flow and share your gifts? What would that feel like?

Another coaching client shared this on social media:

"I am a first-generation college graduate. When I was attending school I lacked familial support while navigating the other struggles any first-gen student would experience. Knowing that if I overcame these struggles, I would be able to one day advocate for others, was enough to spark my motivation to pursue my degrees. It was difficult to land where I am now.

"I was offered limited resources from my family and school. Connecting with individuals, such as peers and mentors, who share similar struggles was an important navigation tool, and I advise you all to do the same. Do not be afraid to reach out! It is important for you all to not only find that motivation, but discover your interests! Consistency is not quick, but the results are always evident."

Internal Contemplation

1. How can you slow down in your life?

2. Where can you eliminate a task that you don't need to do?

3. What are you creating right now?

External Action

When you feel behind, or overwhelmed, slow down your breath and your movements. Notice how that affects your creativity.

Chapter 6

Principle Three: Centering

If you have no confidence in self,

you are twice defeated in the race of life.

– Marcus Garvey

As a lawyer, you likely don't give in easily. You probably don't accept things the way they are. You use your position of power to help others.

Being powerful, to a lawyer, often means an aggressive overtaking of others. When you do this, you're actually giving up your power to assert control over those around you. Unfortunately, this method will pull you out of integrity. Your leadership has to come from a place of stable confidence. If you aggressively drag people into doing things the way you want, you're not centered in yourself. Centering means trusting yourself to your core. When you trust yourself, others can trust you.

Remember Dale Carnegie's iconic *How to Win Friends and Influence People*? As a teenager, I was horrified that people were praising a book that manipulates people into being your friends. The ethics of the situation disturbed this future lawyer. It wasn't until later that I realized that there are skills to be learned for how to communicate in a way that draws people to me naturally. I can influence people from a centered place. I don't have to aggressively chase people in order for them to follow me.

Your third principle of lawyer leadership is developing the skill of influencing by centering yourself instead of arguing. The job title of influencer is really popular right now in social media. But do you want to overwhelm others with your message, or do you want to share your authentic opinion? It's one thing to provide content. It's another thing to actually affect people on a lasting basis. You want to influence people through your message, to guide them on their own journey.

On *The New Billable Hour Podcast,* I share my views and lessons from my own journey. While I give my own perspective, the listener sees it through their lens of experience. I am impressed with how listeners are receiving the information. One of my ongoing listeners explained to me that my podcast is like art, and the listener will take what they need from it.

> "Leadership is having and holding a vision to the exclusion of other things, and taking action toward that end in a way that inspires and motivates other people to join you and support you."
>
> – Lawyer Leader Interview

This lawyer leader principle invites you to find your center, the very core of your being, to find your power. By grounding into your center, you can express yourself from a calm place. When you come from a calm and powerful center, you can influence others.

One of my coaching clients makes sure they are grounded when they meet with clients, have a court appearance, or are about to give a presentation. They breathe deeply and connect with their center to find calmness. They have collected many mindfulness tools that help them when they feel imbalanced or ungrounded. Then, from that grounded place, they can access more of themself and not get caught up in stress or fear.

However, for you, that stress may motivate you to serve. The stress that comes from imbalance may ignite your passion and your courage to argue against the status quo. Argument is an essential skill of lawyering. Arguing well is an important part of your identity as a lawyer. Perhaps you even enjoy it. You may love the challenge, the intellectual stimulation, and the sheer creativity of it.

As a lawyer, you get to use the power of discourse to communicate with other intelligent people about life-changing situations. You create law and evolve legal theories with your persuasion. This is what attracted you to this complicated profession. You are a staunch advocate unafraid to make an argument, be it oral or written.

While argument is the basis of our legal system, you know that method is only one tool for practicing law. Unfortunately, you may rely on this tool in all areas of your life. You may create arguments when they're not necessary and use aggressive tactics to force others to back down. Life (and leadership) is not about who's the strongest in physical or intellectual strength. While strength may have been useful to succeed in school and the workplace, there are consequences of overexertion.

When you rely on strength or argument to handle conflict and express yourself, you are operating from a place of reaction. You are not operating from your center, from that calm, knowing place. When you shift to a nonviolent, purpose-driven source of power, possibilities expand. New options surface, and people listen to you.

When people truly listen and trust you, they are automatically influenced. You may even give them the message they've been looking for, and it will literally bring tears to their eyes.

> "Leadership is being able to lead by example, and not just saying you should act a certain way or do things a certain way. But, being the role model that everybody should follow, and actually caring about your team. I have heard that a manager pushes from behind, and a true leader from the front. A good analogy I heard is that Julius Caesar, when he went to battle, wasn't typically behind his troops as most generals would be. He would ride up front."
>
> – Lawyer Leader Interview

In your law practice, it may seem that you're constantly trying to convince others of your position. Whether it be the judge or jury, opposing counsel, or your client, you may feel desperate in pushing your agenda.

But you may also be tired of being so aggressive. Deep down, you know that you are not an aggressive person. You are merely trying to fit the role of the powerful attorney that you and others expect. When you can calmly connect with yourself on a core level, you become a better advocate for your clients.

There is a different way to lawyer than what you have been taught. There is a way that doesn't require you to drop any of your beloved qualities, but instead builds on them in a way that will make you more organized in your role as leader and influencer. In aikido, my teachers constantly reminded me of the foundation quote from our founder Morihei Ueshiba (O-Sensei): "True victory is victory over one's self."

My interpretation of this aikido quote is that even though we are practicing a martial art with others, we are doing it to get to know ourselves. As we know ourselves, we can then learn how to be with others. In a literal sense, in this martial art, the intention is to get our partner (not opponent) in a position so that we have the same point of view. We get there by paying attention to our center.

We maintain heightened awareness of our center so that no matter what the other is doing, we are the one influencing, not being distracted by an external attack.

When we come from a grounded, calm center, the response, "I don't know" is the right answer when we actually don't know.

> "For me, leadership used to mean being the person who knew the most in the room, and telling people what to do, or sharing my knowledge with others. And then, over time, it has evolved into something that is quieter, and involves helping other people succeed without necessarily simultaneously promoting myself. I am actually doing things to help people in their careers without needing to get a lot of noise or credit about it. I am moving into a space of more confidence. I see that through quiet diplomacy I can really help others get where they want to go."
>
> – Lawyer Leader Interview

If you're tired of doing everything the same way and getting the same results, explore practicing law differently. You'll get better results for everyone.

Internal Contemplation

1. Think of a leader or influential person who gave a speech that really moved you. Embody that feeling.

2. What are your personal core values?

3. What does it feel like when you are out of integrity?

External Action

Create a document with the core values of your law practice.

Chapter 7

Principle Four: Vulnerability

There is no passion to be found playing small –

in settling for a life that is less

than the one you are capable of living.

– Nelson Mandela

The world is in a precarious place right now. We are a litigious society looking to blame others for the intense suffering we experience. As lawyers, we have been pulled into this emotional setup from the beginning of our careers. Humans created the conflict and blame, and lawyers perpetuate it.

I respect and honor our legal system the way it is. I am grateful for the opportunities it has given lawyers to help clients and make change. I also offer an alternative to how we see our role as lawyers in the system we have created.

What if we were more heart-centered in addressing conflict? What if we led our clients, opposing counsel, judges, and the general public from a place of connection? What if lawyers were the ones to actually heal the world of its conflict?

This lawyer leader principle is the turning point to elevate your level of leadership. You removed your lawyer mask, slowed down, and found your center. Now it's time to put yourself out there. Vulnerability means allowing others to see your true self.

Opening my own heart has been a challenge for me. I mistakenly learned early on in my life that having an open heart was a dangerous thing. I perceived being vulnerable as opening myself up to hurt. Accordingly, I brilliantly put armor around my heart to protect it.

With that barrier in place, I could move around in the world with more safety by arming myself. This strategy helped me manage, and even succeed, in many ways. This armor also created a scaffolding to protect my heart and avoid being vulnerable.

I chose the legal profession as a way to help others who are in vulnerable positions. I stand up for my clients and advocate for them when they can't do it for themselves. With a protected heart, I have become resilient to withstand adversity. While this strategy has worked for me so far, it is time to peel away those barriers.

I have achieved as much success as I could with a guarded heart. In order to go further and get unstuck, I need to do something differently. Can you relate? In order for me to lead on a deeper level, I must expose my vulnerability. I must let go of my barriers and let my light shine through. I share this with you, lawyer leader, because I am inviting you to do the same in this principle.

> "As lawyers, we are trained to perform for our clients. It's a performative, posturing profession historically. There are interesting parallels for me in the way I've also performed gender or womanhood. For me, being an attorney has also allowed me to put on armor around other, more vulnerable places,

such as being gender queer."

– Lawyer Leader Interview

When you allow yourself to be vulnerable, you open your heart to feel all your emotions. When you think about emotions, you may imagine the worst of them. You may think about the ups and downs, the sideways, the ways that your feelings interfere with seeing clearly. However, there are many different kinds of emotions. Some emotions, such as empathy and joy, can serve you well. While other emotions, such as anger and hurt, can get in your way if you dwell in them.

Feel those negative emotions, and then let them go. Serve others authentically by healing yourself. Emotions are not the enemy, but what you do with them can be. Your strong emotions indicate imbalance. If you are constantly in an aggressively protective posture, then you will stay in reactive mode. This mode will lead to burnout.

To get out of that reactive state so that you can respond calmly, you must embrace your emotional intelligence. Learn to feel. Your neglected feelings can get in the way of your logical brain thinking. In my previous book, *The Holistic Lawyer*, I offer a system to help you connect head, heart, and gut through engagement in tools to expand your abilities beyond your intellect.

In that book, I describe how you may limit your intelligence by staying solely in your head. You must also connect with your body, your heart and emotions, and your gut and intuition. These other brain centers, intentionally accessed, can make life a lot easier. When you fully integrate all the parts of you, you can see beyond what you thought possible.

> "People have a tendency to push things downwards and feel like it's someone else's problem. But if you are truly leading, then it's your problem – everything is your problem. It's complete ownership rather than hiding from it or fleeing from it."
>
> – Lawyer Leader Interview

As a holistic lawyer, you become smarter overall through emotional intelligence, which is accessed by opening your heart. As you learn to master matters of the heart, you can lead from a place of connection and love.

In this book I invite you, lawyer leader, to lead from your heart. By leading from a place of connection and love, you set up the best scenario to make lasting change.

You know about the modern strategies and tactics to get ahead and further your career. There are always new ideas being born. But when you chase after the latest shiny object, you lose sight of what's important. You lose sight of your core values and the reason you are doing this at all.

You know what happens when you don't have purpose – you can suffer from a meaningless, empty life. Things may look great on the outside: income, family, and possessions. But inside there's that feeling that there must be something more.

When you lead others (and yourself) from your heart, you start with your inner purpose and radiate that outward. You create what you want to see in your world.

> "We are more than just our jobs; we are more than attorneys; we are human beings. We have feelings; we have aspirations, goals, and dreams."
>
> – Lawyer Leader Interview

The process of increasing your emotional intelligence to access more of your heart is a valuable one. At first, I myself did not want to do this work. But since I decided to take the plunge (with the help of mentors, after my own personal development work and psychotherapy), my life and work have only become more successful.

As a lawyer leader, the time is ripe for you to open up your heart. One way to actively open your heart is to become an observer of your feelings. Imagine your individual feelings in a pile in the middle of the room. From a distance, feel the feelings all the way through, and then release them. Remember that the way to help others access their heart centers is to activate your own. You will draw out the kindness and goodwill of others by being sincere yourself.

> "I recently learned about my need for appreciation. I'm learning to detach from that need so that I can love and give more freely without assigning the responsibility of appreciation to others who didn't ask for that assignment."
>
> – Lawyer Leader Interview

Allowing yourself to become vulnerable does not mean being an overly emotional leader. In fact, when you truly lead from your heart your emotions are even-keeled. You feel compassion but are not fatigued by it. You feel anger, but you're not overcome by it. You feel sadness, but you're not weakened by it. You feel your emotions instead of burying them, and they cannot sway you from your role as leader.

I believe with all my heart that you as a lawyer are positioned to be a leader. By being more heart-centered, you can ignite your leadership skills to bring those around you (and those around them) to a better place. Are you ready to open your heart and be more vulnerable? In vulnerability lies immense power. Use this power to create change in the world.

Internal Contemplation

1. When do you feel most vulnerable?

2. How are you arming yourself for protection?

3. How can you safely open up more?

External Action

Find out your emotional IQ and specific ways to increase it. *Note:* You can find several tools online. Search "emotional intelligence" or "emotional IQ."

Chapter 8

Principle Five: Communication

In recognizing the humanity

of our fellow beings,

we pay ourselves the highest tribute.

– Thurgood Marshall

Despite what we may think, lawyers don't always communicate clearly. This is because we are taught not to. We hide behind legalese and use language that's convoluted instead of direct. Two lawyers in opposition can generate unnecessarily aggressive legal communication. This communication style can be passed on as permission for our clients to engage in immature, violent speech.

> "As a lawyer, leadership means upholding ideals of our profession. It means being civil and responsible and professional and ethical. When lawyers engage in violent communication between us, we are teaching our clients who are learning to communicate. I will not participate, and I call other lawyers out on it."
>
> – Lawyer Leader Interview

Communication is complicated; words are limited. You may mean to express one thing, and the listener hears a completely different message. As you articulate your message, you must be cognizant of its external impact. Have you had the experience of perceiving your message to be so clear that you couldn't believe that anyone could misunderstand you?

A medium-sized law firm recently hired me as their productivity consultant. A partner at this law firm was frustrated because they believed they were perfectly clear about explaining law firm procedure to staff. However, some of the staff were not following procedure. The partner concluded the problem was with the staff members. But after digging into the communication problem with me, they were able to see that the firm's policies needed to be more explicit.

Communication within a law firm, especially with non-lawyer staff, is challenging. In managing my own law firm, I often thought I was being crystal clear in my communication with staff and clients. When my message was not received as intended, I insisted that it was the other person's fault, and that they just didn't get it. It took me many conflicts and difficult conversations to finally realize the problem was actually with me. I needed to better understand my own communication style.

I realized that no matter how clear I think I am, the only way to communicate my point of view is to be even clearer. In communication seminars, I have often been taught that communication means both sending and receiving. If my message isn't received and understood, it's a failed communication. It is my responsibility to make sure my communications are understood.

The fifth principle for you, the lawyer leader, is to take responsibility for what and how you communicate with others. This responsibility begins with putting more effort into listening than speaking. Cultivate the practice of listening to those around you.

> "A skill that a lot of leaders lack is to listen to what people are saying and not having the need to react or respond necessarily, because not everyone wants a reaction or response. They just want to be heard."
> – Lawyer Leader Interview

Learn to listen carefully to your own inner voice. By removing your extra commentary and defensiveness, you can more clearly express yourself. You may be inadvertently clouding your point of view with fear of how it will be received. You may add irrelevant information, and you may distract the other from actually understanding what you are saying.

Fear can also make you back off from your communication and trigger your desire to please others. You may be afraid to upset other people with your truth. What if you allowed the other person to really understand where you were coming from, from your vulnerable point of view?

> "I am outspoken; I don't mind asking for what it is I want or need. A person has to have that, whether it

was developed as you were growing up, or whether you did it as an adult because you had to."

– Lawyer Leader Interview

If your point is not received, be clearer. I am not saying to be condescending and talk down to others. To the contrary, I am saying to be humble and talk up to your audience. Give them more credit. Offer them your truth in a way they can hear it. This requires that you be vulnerable and humble. Instead of trying to justify your result, as you may do in a brief or legal argument, express yourself directly. Answer questions that are asked, and be honest in your responses.

When I first started in aikido, I started training exercises from a posture of tension. My partner would come at me with their energy. If I met that force with equally opposing energy, we would both be stuck. While I could use brute force to overtake my partner, such action would be temporary. Instead, adhering to aikido philosophy, I continuously practiced moving my partner and myself to both face the same direction. This meant we would be safely out of the combat posture.

When we both had the same point of view, we could blend (or communicate) without resistance. Aikido is a beautiful art form to learn how to communicate. I have transferred this art to my own leadership skills. Instead of forcing my point of view onto others, I focus on expressing my truth in an effective and nonviolent way.

Nonviolent communication, or NVC, was developed by clinical psychologist Marshall Rosenberg. His approach focuses on meeting the needs of all parties involved in a communication. Most basically, the model is to move away from coercive speech to a more cooperative approach of self-expression and empathic listening.

I invite you to bring this model into your communication as a lawyer leader. Be more honest and authentic in expressing yourself. Evolve yourself from the traditional premise that lawyers are experts and know better than others. You may believe you know best what others need. Truth is, you probably do know. But must you communicate that?

I understand how you would want to communicate that knowing, and beyond. I have even thought that I was helping people by overpowering them. This tendency can become controlling behavior. Instead of dominating others so I can feel heard, I have learned to allow them to openly receive my communication.

"Lawyers get this stereotype for making things harder, but we keep people honest. We are truth tellers; we seek after the truth."

– Lawyer Leader Interview

As a lawyer, your role as truth teller cannot be taken lightly. Even if you mean well deep down, you can cause harm to others with your unsophisticated communication. Further, you can burn yourself out trying to control others instead of meeting them where they are. This skill of simplifying your communication by listening to others, listening to yourself, and expressing yourself clearly is a benchmark for how well you can lead.

Internal Contemplation

1. What is your biggest challenge with communicating with others? Is it different with different groups – i.e., clients, opposing counsel, judges?

2. How can you simplify your communication so it will be clearer?

3. If you could only communicate one thing to the world, what would that be?

External Action

Research the Four-Step Process of Nonviolent Communication, and try to use it in your conversations. (www.nonviolentcommunication.com/learn-nonviolent-communication/4-part-nvc/)

Chapter 9

Principle Six: Self-Integration

You can't be what you can't see.

– Marian Wright Edelman

Mature leaders are genuinely strong, centered, and productive. When you reorganize yourself in a more centered way, you become more structured and calmer. In other words, when you mature, you get yourself together! From this inner structure, you can create outer change.

In my previous book, *The Holistic Lawyer*, I explain how to integrate your *brain* by connecting with your emotional and gut intelligence. However, integrating your *soul* requires you to go deeper into your psyche. This is a psychological and spiritual journey to connect all the parts of your being.

The use of archetypes can help you organize yourself in a concrete way. An archetype is a pattern or model that you can emulate. In Jungian psychology, archetypes are characters that recur so frequently in myths and stories that they suggest their experiences are universal.

You have the capacity to embody the roles of these characters. By getting in touch with all the parts of yourself, you can lead more fully. Self-integration is the sixth principle of lawyer leadership.

The archetype lawyers are most familiar with is Justitia, usually portrayed as Lady Justice. She is a well-known symbol of our justice system and can be found depicted widely in courthouses and law firms.

In one hand Lady Justice holds scales, which represent weighing of evidence and balance. In her other hand she holds a double-edged sword, for both enforcement and defense of the law. Justitia's blindfold stands for objectivity in the legal system.

Justice is blind, but you as a lawyer leader can see that is it far more complicated than that. The world has changed much since the legal system was initially created. As I have stated earlier, the legal system is slow to change. As a lawyer leader, you fight within the system to create change. You can take on this role authentically while maintaining your calm and stability.

You may mistake controlling, threatening, and hostile behaviors for strength. You may also think of vulnerability as weakness. You need both types of energies in order to be successful. You must be able to take initiative and be aggressive when needed. The role of a lawyer is to take action to stand up and fight for someone, or something, worth your efforts.

Do not give up the good fight. But make sure you have all the tools to fight effectively. This book and these principles are designed to help you be a better lawyer while you lead your colleagues to a better way of lawyering.

In my earlier books, I emphasize that the path to productivity and working smarter is finding balance. An imbalanced life can lead to difficulties. The overly aggressive lawyer is one of the most important imbalances to be addressed in order to move our profession forward.

Excessive aggressiveness covers up deep insecurities. My own lawyer journey began with low self-confidence. When I started coaching other lawyers, I found this to be the case for all of my clients, regardless of their gender, race, ethnic background, upbringing, age, or even experience. Lawyers constantly battle with feeling disempowered and inferior because they are trusted with the responsibility to make important decisions for others.

It is natural to cover up those insecure feelings with inflation and arrogance. The feelings may also lead to perfectionism and its close sibling, procrastination. When you allow those inferior feelings to block parts of yourself, you can become a helpless victim.

You have to constantly work to connect with your center, which is creative and vital. From there, you can wield your influence and weapons positively. You can only truly lead if you have a sense of your own worthiness that comes from your center.

You can connect with your role as a spiritual warrior. Whether oral or written, you are driven to fight to prove your point to someone else. In addition, you also need to connect with your compassion and vulnerability. By being vulnerable, you open yourself to what could be; you open up possibilities.

You can see how things *could* be instead of constantly fighting for how things *should* be. Vulnerability is the new power position. If you are confident enough to allow information and perspectives to pierce your veil, you can see more clearly what needs to be done and how to do it.

> "Leadership is both knowing what you are doing, and the humility to realize that you may not have all the answers or be the only person who has any relevant input. There may be others in your group who will have valuable input, and even better ideas than you. Leadership is a position of strength; you don't feel threatened by somebody who is working for you to give input on how you do things."
>
> – Lawyer Leader Interview

Cultivate your ability to receive ideas, perspectives, and insights that come from outside. Look from the point of view of someone you are having a conflict with – opposing counsel, judge, or client. Try to understand what they're going through with empathy and emotional intelligence. Start with seeing that the other person's view is different from yours or your client's.

There is strength in allowing others to be different from you and not seeking to aggressively change them. How can this idea help you be a lawyer leader? In order to lead from those higher levels of leadership I discuss at the beginning of this book, you must be able to take in other perspectives so you can understand the situations you face.

> "Leadership is a collaborative effort. It is sharing what I bring to the table and learning from others around me. It is functioning as a mentor, providing guidance, refinement, or instruction as the needs suit themselves. A leader is someone who can impart knowledge and can absorb knowledge."
>
> – Lawyer Leader Interview

Modern culture is about the individual instead of the collective. Western civilization pushes you to strike out on your own. You are supposed to be self-reliant, but lack the resources to take full responsibility for your actions. By integrating yourself into a mature leader, you can be ready for what comes.

As a lawyer, you are trained to crush any other perspective. You have your truth and are willing to present it in a way that will destroy your opponent. This is the definition of a bulldog lawyer. You are expected to do this even if you don't agree with the truth you are working with.

Let's hold onto the confidence of the bulldog, and just add in the sensitivity of … say … a poodle? Please excuse my lack of knowledge about dogs, but you get the point, I hope.

By embracing the power of vulnerability and receptivity, you can expand your net of awareness. Instead of pounding hard on getting your point across, you step back and let the other points frame your point in a way that can be heard. Look at the big picture to make a difference with your expertise.

> "Leadership is a collaborative thing for me; that's how I view when I am in charge of anything. I see how other people can help me to accomplish this, although I am, in name, the leader."
>
> – Lawyer Leader Interview

Collaboration, communication, creative solutions, mediation, alternative dispute resolution, and specialty interdisciplinary court systems are all part of the new wave of the legal profession. Where is your role in this new wave? Where do you belong as a lawyer leader who wants to make a difference in people's lives? Do you feel that the aggressive energy you have used is not enough anymore? If so, I invite you to welcome in a more expansive way of using your expertise as a lawyer. I invite you to integrate yourself to live more fully and lead more completely.

Internal Contemplation

1. How do you emphasize your aggressive energy in order to succeed as a lawyer?
2. Why is it important to use that initiative to fight for your client?
3. Where can you incorporate more collaboration into your law practice and life?

External Action

Create a process in your law practice for how you can be more receptive to different perspectives and accept input different from your own.

Chapter 10

Principle Seven: Presence

I believe unconditionally in the ability of people to respond when they are told the truth. We need to be taught to study rather than believe, to inquire rather than to affirm.

– Septima Poinsette Clark

Advancement in information technology and artificial intelligence is taking great strides. Mass-marketed, do-it-yourself legal options loom as threats to the lawyer's livelihood, profession, and identity. I worry about the future of law and your place in it.

The legal profession is flawed, as I have been expounding upon in my books. Lawyers are reluctant to fix it because it's based on tradition, and any change can be painfully slow. But I have a shortcut that can bring you results right now.

The seventh and final principle for lawyer leadership will change the paradigm of law and reclaim your future. The future of law is being present. Finding presence in your daily life is the path to future change.

In his book *Lawyer Forward*, Mike Whelan invites lawyers to stop churning and start using the expertise we uniquely hold. Whelan sets out a new way of lawyering that focuses on using our abilities to think strategically, analyze, and form opinions based on different scenarios. If we can shift away from the current model of lawyering, which is leading to burnout, we can change the trajectory for what we do and how we do it.

"Leadership in the legal profession has a lot to do with our willingness to accept change. There are

> so many people who think that because that's the way it has always been done, that is the way it has to be done."
>
> – Lawyer Leader Interview

What can you do right now, at this moment, to improve your future as a lawyer and the futures of those you lead? Anxiety and stress come from worrying about a future you cannot know. It's natural to be stressed about it. Trying to imagine the future from a stressful present will result in doomsday scenarios.

However, if you can be aware of what's happening in the moment, you can create a future that is sustainable and even enjoyable. As you have been doing the exercises and creating tools for each principle in this book, you have been honing your ability to slow down, pay attention, and cultivate more space in your life.

Now is the time to tie it all together and, from your new place of presence, create your own future. By doing that, you are creating the future for those you lead.

> "You don't have to be the loudest person in the room; you don't have to be the funniest person in the room, continually just show up."
>
> – Lawyer Leader Interview

Here is where I wish I could literally tell you what to do, how to do it, and whom to lead. But it doesn't work that way. I cannot even begin to know what your role and purpose is now, or in the future. Only you can know by settling down in the present, calling in what you want the future to be, and working toward that future with purpose. This shift will help you, your colleagues, your clients, opposing counsel, and judges to embrace a future of law that will emphasize the role of lawyers as leaders.

> "Leadership is having and holding a vision to the exclusion of other things, and taking action towards that end in a way that inspires and motivates other people to join you and support you."
>
> – Lawyer Leader Interview

What the world needs right now is for you to be present and prepare for your future by going inward.

I coached a successful lawyer with numerous accomplishments, including managing their own firm, steadily increasing revenue, and engaging more high-end clients they loved to work with. While this lawyer's exterior world looked great, on the inside, no matter how much they achieved, they dwelled on what they had *not* done and feared loss of success. They felt they were always in second place, never first. This lawyer had difficulty being present. They were unable to stop anxious thoughts about the future.

We explored what first place would feel like for them. They felt it when in flow and absorbed in a case, training for a marathon, and being with cherished friends. These glimpses of first place meant being present in the moment and feeling so powerful they could do anything.

First place is simply putting yourself first. That is what being present means. I am sure you have felt it, even if the feeling was fleeting. If you practice mindfulness over time, you will increasingly feel it in all parts of your life. If you've just started being mindful, you may not feel it just yet. I promise it is coming.

Like any muscle, strengthening your ability to notice what you are doing and what is coming up requires practice. But it should not be hard or onerous. This opportunity, to be present to what is, turns out to be a gift that keeps giving.

By opening yourself up to the here and now from acceptance and curiosity, you are practicing. You have done this process with the first six lawyer leadership principles. Now you can keep practicing so that you feel present more often than not. Before you know it, another world opens up to you.

You will see the future as merely an extension of the present. You will see that the future is not to be feared but to be created by you. The future of law is contained in the present. Every moment lived is setting yourself up for what's next.

If you make choices that are out of integrity, those choices will negatively influence future choices. If you constantly compromise your values and morals out of fear of not fitting in, your future will be based on fear. However, if you try to make subtle changes and improvements to how you show up for the law, those actions will create new paths and possibilities.

How you behave and engage right now with your work and life is creating your future. Since you are called to so much more than just churning out cases, the future of law depends on you.

The feeling of placing yourself first builds the foundation for something grand. The only person who can do this for you is you. How will this idea change how you practice law, prioritize your life, and claim your identity?

There is no time to wallow in the frustration of the law not changing. Lawyer leader, now is your time to shine. Now is the time to be in this exact moment and claim the future of law for you and everyone else. Being present is your future in law.

Internal Contemplation

1. Why is being a lawyer an important part of your identity?
2. What does being present feel like for you?
3. How are the first six principles helping you open up to the present?

External Action

Write a different kind of vision statement. Describe the future you want to create for yourself, the legal profession, and those you lead. Share it widely.

Chapter 11

Ethical Responsibility

Each person must live

their life as a model for others.

– Rosa Parks

You take your responsibilities as a lawyer seriously. But you also have an unrealistic expectation of your own capacity. You want to meet the highest standards and impossible best practices in all you do. This perfectionism can hold you back.

I hope that engaging with the seven principles of lawyer leadership in this book has smoothed your edges, so you can see beyond the false illusion of perfection. It is my intention to help you release some beliefs that you have held so tightly as a lawyer. There was good reason for holding them. Now I invite you to consider letting them go, or at least loosening your grip – even though these beliefs created your identity as a lawyer.

Just like you, I also hold these beliefs close to me. While I have many professional roles, my identity is foremost a lawyer, and I introduce myself that way. I cannot support other lawyers in embracing themselves if I am not true to myself. Being a lawyer is such a core identity that only another lawyer can understand.

As lawyers, our self-confidence is not stable. It depends on how things are going around us. We can't always feel self-assured. Likewise, in transitioning to a more confident leadership role, we will often regress to feeling incompetent. Unfortunately, this is the torch we bear as lawyer leaders. We are creating change for those coming after us.

Like most change movements, this one starts by each of us acknowledging that what we have been doing is not working anymore. Further, what we have been doing is hurting us and those around us. Once we can acknowledge that, then we can change it.

Change starts with you.

You may still be concerned that you will make mistakes. Of course you will make mistakes. With this new way, there are fewer rules and milestone markers. It is akin to traveling in the pathless woods. We are bushwhacking a new trail, while there are others behind us ready to follow.

Several years ago, I participated in a backpacking trip in the Escalante National Monument in Utah. We were cross-country hiking without trails. We slogged inside a stream and bushwhacked our way into the most radiant, bright orange rock formations I had ever seen. These places were practically untouched by other humans.

The trip was not a smooth effort, though. We were traveling in a group and needed to look after each other. There was one hiker who was extremely dehydrated, and we had to slow down to accommodate them. Several times after river crossings that involved climbing down a bank with a heavy pack on my back and then climbing up the opposite bank, we had to retrace our steps. Our knowledgeable trip leaders had to be flexible and change course regularly.

This goes to show that no matter how much we plan, we have to adjust our actions accordingly.

When we as lawyer leaders can be brave enough to go off trail and create a new path, we make it up as we go. We backtrack when needed. We change our speed to accommodate our followers. We keep going. We lean on each other. We have a good time and relish the beauty of the journey.

In my own lawyer leader journey, I have had many mentors guide me along the way. We all need mentors who are just enough ahead of us that we follow them with trust. We know they've already seen the beautiful camping spot and that they want to take us there.

Maybe the journey will be slightly different this time because of overgrowth and rainfall. But the leaders are committed to find that next place, taking into consideration who is following them.

You are that leader and mentor.

While mentors help keep you moving forward, you keep those behind you moving forward as well. Mentors can see your blind spots and help you face them. As you mentor and lead others, it is important to have your own community and mentors. When you open up your heart and mind, there is a danger that the extreme weight of the world can swallow you.

Being vulnerable in the world today is a delicate expedition and should not be taken lightly. Please join and create communities where you feel safe to be you, and use mentors to guide you in the right direction. Since you have come this far in the journey, there is no turning back.

It is your legacy to ethically leave the legal profession better than when you joined it. You have an ethical responsibility to lead the profession to its next level. Your profession is unique in that you hold strong to your ethics above all else. Ethical responsibilities often make you anxious because it can feel like you are deficient. But ethics are what keep you focused. As you learn your ethical rules, you adapt and change how you practice law.

Your lawyer journey is much like your leadership journey. Being on a journey means you are present to the challenge that is right in front of you. You are grateful for the opportunity to learn and grow.

Your ethical responsibility to lead the legal profession to its next stage of evolution starts with leading yourself. By reading this book, you have already taken the first step.

Final Contemplation

1. Which principle do you feel like you are naturally good at? How will you use that principle in your leadership?

2. Which principle is the most difficult for you? How can you focus on growing in that area?

3. In six months from now, where will you be in your leadership journey? How will you treat yourself? How will you treat others?

Final Action

Find colleagues, community, and mentors to support you on your journey.

Conclusion

I have always thought that what is needed is the development of people who are interested not in being leaders as much as in developing leadership in others.

– Ella Baker

Lawyers are the leaders of our time. This book is meant to be the catalyst for a lawyer leader movement. Lawyers are modern-day warriors on the front lines.

We negotiate conflict. We counsel those who have been harmed. We stand up for the marginalized people of our society. We speak up for fairness and justice. We ethically protect human and civil rights and push to expand them. When lawyers speak, we are listened to.

It's time to take this responsibility to the next level. Society needs leaders who are intelligent negotiators, mediators, and problem-solvers.

Dear lawyer, the time is now to use your unique training and authoritative position to take on this leadership role. It is time to bring all of yourself to this present moment. Leadership is about bringing all of you to the forefront so that you can serve others and make a deep impact.

The highest levels of leadership – Catalyst, Co-creator, and Synergist – are accessible to you if you consistently practice the seven principles described in this book.

Principle One: Authenticity

Authenticity is the degree to which your actions are congruent with your beliefs and desires, despite external pressures. Imposter syndrome cannot exist if you are being true to yourself.

Principle Two: Creativity

You can create lasting change by moving slowly. This requires confidence in yourself. It requires acceptance of all the unfinished tasks in your life right now.

Principle Three: Centering

By grounding into your center, you can express yourself from a calm place. When you come from a steady and powerful center, you can influence others.

Principle Four: Vulnerability

When you are vulnerable, you connect with your heart. Heart-centered lawyering means opening yourself up to feeling all emotions.

Principle Five: Communication

Be clear in your communication. Be humble and talk up to your audience. Give them more credit. Offer them your truth in a way they can hear.

Principle Six: Self-integration

When you access your orderliness within, you will get yourself together. Cultivate your ability to receive the ideas, perspectives, and insights that come from outside.

Principle Seven: Presence

First place is simply putting yourself first. That is what being present means. If you practice mindfulness over time, you will increasingly feel it in all parts of your life.

These seven lawyer leader principles are your foundation for mature leadership. This is the blueprint for you to make a shift, so that your colleagues and the profession can shift. Your personal shift will reverberate out to those all around you – your clients, colleagues, opposing counsel, judges, clerks, and the general public.

Together all lawyer leaders will change the reputation and image of lawyers. Lawyer leaders, like you, will bring the ideal of authentic service to our profession, and create global change by finding our collective inner peace.

Further Reading

Action Inquiry: The Secret of Timely and Transforming Leadership by William R. Torbert

Appreciative Inquiry: A Positive Revolution in Change by David L. Cooperrider and Diana Whitney

HBR's 10 Must Reads on Leadership by Harvard Business Review

Journey to the Heart of Aikido: The Teachings of Motomichi Anno Sensei by Linda Holiday

King Warrior Magician Lover: Rediscovering the Archetypes of the Mature Masculine by Robert Moore and Douglas Gillette

Lawyer Forward: Finding Your Place in the Future of Law by Mike Whelan, Jr.

Leadership Agility: Five Levels of Mastery for Anticipating and Initiating Change by Bill Joiner and Stephen Josephs

Leadership on the Leading Edge: Shift Your Life and Work Up to the Highest Levels by Dr. Ron Stotts

Nonviolent Communication: A Language of Life: Life-Changing Tools for Healthy Relationships by Marshall B. Rosenberg, PhD

The Holistic Lawyer: Use Your Whole Brain to Work Smarter Not Harder by Ritu Goswamy, Esq.

The New Billable Hour: Bill More Hours, Be More Productive, and Still Have Work-Life Balance by Ritu Goswamy, Esq.

Acknowledgments

Thank you to Maggie McReynolds and the Un-Settling Books team for bringing my vision of this book to life! I appreciate your guidance for the transformational experience this book has been for me.

Thank you to Dr. Ron Stotts for introducing me to the leadership research.

Thank you to Chief Instructor Linda Holiday and all the teachers and students at Aikido of Santa Cruz for guiding me on my leadership path.

To the lawyers who trusted me and signed up for the first lawyer leader mentorship program before I had created it: Parag Amin, Yvette Saddik Jimenez, and Amita Vasudeva. Thank you for your vulnerability and self-leadership.

I feel deep gratitude for the lawyers who volunteered to participate in lawyer leader interviews with me. I quote only a fraction of those actual conversations in this book, but those interactions shaped the direction of the book and its message in many ways. Thank you for leading the way with your confidence and willingness to contribute to this project.

Sincere appreciation to all my coaching clients, especially the ones quoted in this book. You keep me humble and committed to moving forward in this work.

Finally I thank all my teachers, coaches, mentors, supervisors, colleagues, and friends who have led me and taught me how to lead myself.

Next Step

Dear Lawyer Leader,

By reading this book, you have already begun your lawyer leadership journey. Next is to find mentors and community to support your progress.

If you would like to connect with me about mentorship and/or community options, please visit my website at www.ritugoswamy.com to schedule an initial consultation.

Looking forward to meeting you,
Ritu

About the Author

RITU GOSWAMY, ESQ., is a Lawyer Leader Coach and DEI (Diversity, Equity, and Inclusion) Strategist for law firms. Ritu is the best-selling author of *The New Billable Hour: Bill More Hours, Be More Productive, and Still Have Work Life Balance* and *The Holistic Lawyer: Use Your Whole Brain to Work Smarter Not Harder.*

Ritu created the New Billable Hour®, the Holistic Lawyer, and the Lawyer Leader online courses and coaching programs. They host *The New Billable Hour Podcast,* available where you like to listen and on YouTube.

Ritu coaches lawyers individually and in groups, consults with law firms, and is an active speaker and trainer in the areas of lawyer leadership, well-being, competency, mindfulness, inclusion, and elimination of bias.

Ritu works remotely from their home office in the Santa Cruz Mountains in California and travels the world to work with clients.

Website: ritugoswamy.com
LinkedIn: ritu-goswamy
Facebook: RituGoswamyEsq
Instagram: @ritugoswamy
Twitter: @ritugoswamy

About the Author

[illegible]

Made in the USA
Monee, IL
04 November 2026

67380805R00075